THE
UNIVERSITY
IN
TRANSITION

THE STAFFORD LITTLE LECTURES

PRINCETON UNIVERSITY

The University in Transition

By JAMES A. PERKINS

PRESIDENT, CORNELL UNIVERSITY

PRINCETON, NEW JERSEY

PRINCETON UNIVERSITY PRESS

1966

Copyright © 1966 by Princeton University Press
All Rights Reserved
LC Card: 66-15804
Printed in the United States of America
By Quinn & Boden Company, Inc., Rahway, N.J.

378.73
P449u

FOREWORD

So TIMELY are President Perkins' three lectures on "The University in Transition," delivered at Princeton in the Stafford Little Series, that we believe they should be readily available to interested readers. The lectures constitute an important, clear-sighted analysis, and are ample testimony of the thoughtful and lively leadership Dr. Perkins is exerting in higher education today.

They also testify to the long and friendly relations between Cornell and Princeton, and to the warm esteem in which President Perkins is held here by his many friends and former colleagues.

One may not agree with all of his ideas, or follow all his daring ellipses, but a fair-minded reader must respect the force and cogency of what he has to say, no less than his vigorous expression of it. To all who are concerned with the complex and pressing problems of higher education, as well as to those who seek a readable and lively discussion—so rare in writings on education—we commend these lectures.

ROBERT F. GOHEEN

November 18, 1965

16158

PREFACE

THE READER should know, as he makes his way through these pages, that he is, in effect, joining the audience which gathered in Woodrow Wilson Hall at Princeton University to hear the Stafford Little Lectures in November of 1965. For the lectures are here presented almost exactly as they were delivered. A few minor changes have been made to improve clarity, and a comma or two have been added to improve the punctuation—but nothing more.

More important, however, the reader should be warned that these lectures were meant to be provocative rather than merely descriptive. Many statements could have been rounded off at the edges, and although this might have rendered them more precise, the results would have been less interesting—and perhaps less useful.

In any case, here the lectures are. It is my hope that they will stimulate wiser heads to develop such of these ideas as may have merit and to give better focus to my basic thesis.

In the meantime, some statements of gratitude are in order: to Princeton University for the invitation to give these lectures; to the Rockefeller Foundation for a stay at the Villa Serbelloni and a time to pre-

Preface

pare; to Eric Ashby, Harold Dodds, and Clark Kerr
for their powerful insights into the nature of the
university; to Jean Perkins and Cornell colleagues
for putting up with vacant stares as ideas were being
mentally rearranged; and to John and Barbara
Newsom, without whose help and encouragement
the enterprise might have foundered. In the end,
however, I alone can be held accountable for the
results.

JAMES A. PERKINS

Ithaca, New York
December 1965

CONTENTS

I

THE DYNAMICS
OF
UNIVERSITY
GROWTH

THE DYNAMICS
OF
UNIVERSITY
GROWTH

THE UNIVERSITY has become one of the great institutions of the modern world. In the United States
it is central in the conduct of our national life. It
is the most sophisticated agency we have for advancing knowledge through scholarship and research. It is crucial in the transmittal of knowledge
from one generation to the next. And it is increasingly vital in the application of knowledge to the
problems of modern society. Sir Eric Ashby quotes
from a statement published by the University of
Witwatersrand that makes the point with precision:
" 'Every civilized society tends to develop institutions
which will enable it to acquire, digest, and advance
knowledge relevant to the tasks which, it is thought,

will confront it in the future. Of these institutions, the university is the most important.' "

At the same time, the modern university is, in one of those strange paradoxes of human affairs, dangerously close to becoming the victim of its own success. At a time when there is the greatest clamor among students for admission to the university, there is the greatest dissatisfaction with conditions of student life and studies. At a time when the professions are seeking a broader and more creative role in society, professional education is involving increased attention to the traditional disciplines. At a time when research is richly supported—and respected —it is being described as the academic Trojan horse whose personnel have all but captured the city of the intellect. And at a time when faculty members are in greatest demand for service around the world, there are intimations that their efforts to save the world will cost us our university soul.

How has this paradox come about? What forces are at work? How have they affected the external relations and the internal operations of the university? Can we resist a tendency to internal disorder? Is the university's autonomy and integrity inevitably compromised by its growing involvement with society and by the increasing necessity for state, regional, and national planning?

In the course of these lectures we shall explore

some approaches to these questions, and some tentative answers. And although you may occasionally detect what might appear to be the corruption of a former Princeton graduate student and faculty member by recent experiences as an administrator, I would suggest that there may be offsetting advantages. While I have surrounded myself with the aura of scholarship, and I intend, as a scholar should, to keep as close a grip as possible on the difference between what is and what ought to be, the discussion of the university has now come to the point where theory and doctrine must encounter the practical problems of management and direction. We shall be interested in theory here, but we shall also examine some of the administrative challenges that are being posed in the modern university. We must, after all, find a way to run this extraordinary institution.

Perhaps we should remind ourselves, at the outset, that the university has an ancient and noble ancestry. Its earliest forebears include the Academy of Socrates and the Library of Alexandria, and it shows a line of descent in the Western world that traces the course of civilization. But irrespective of their names, ages, styles, and locations, universities are all what the great German philosopher Karl Jaspers so aptly describes as "the corporate realization of man's basic determination to know." It is here, with knowledge and with man's determination to acquire it, that we must begin. And, as is frequently the case, we must begin with those outsized men, the Greek philosophers of the fifth century B.C., who rise like the columns of their temples out of the plains of early history. For it was these audacious men who dared to suggest that those *determined* to know also had the *capacity* to know; that man, individual man, could by the exercise of his own mind discover truth—not all truth, perhaps, but much truth—about his natural world, his society, and himself.

Others had demonstrated that the realities of the natural world could be grasped better through observation than incantation. The Babylonians believed that to read the mysteries of the world and the universe it was better to observe the trails of stars than the entrails of sheep. But the Greeks did more, far more: they made essential connections among three powerful ideas—that reason could be applied to the results of observation, that knowledge so obtained had a validity apart from things observed, and that this knowledge could be applied to the whole range of human experience.

It would be difficult to overestimate the importance of this Greek affirmation of rational man and the nature of knowledge. Though the world had to wait many centuries for reason to win its major victories, the effects of this affirmation on Western civilization have been decisive. The idea that knowledge could be acquired through logical reasoning laid the groundwork for the whole modern structure which we have built for its pursuit and acquisition. And it gave man a totally different idea of himself which has affected his thought and his action ever since.

But the acquisition of knowledge through the exercise of reason is only part of the story. Knowledge acquired must be transmitted, or it dies. Knowledge acquired and transmitted must be used, or it becomes sterile and inert. Even more, the chemistry of knowledge is such that the very process of transmission, together with the discipline of application, stimulates and guides those who work at the frontiers of knowledge.

Knowledge is, therefore, in many respects a living thing—it grows, it changes, and various of its parts are replaced as they become obsolete. But the dynamic nature of knowledge is traceable to this interplay and tension connected with its acquisition, transmission, and application. It is this interaction that creates needs for new knowledge, that brings inaccurate teaching to account, that shows the world what could be rather than what is. Taken separately the three aspects of knowledge lead nowhere; together they can and have produced an explosion that has changed the world.

Communication has always been the companion of learning. Socrates had a habit of buttonholing people in the street and surrounding himself with students. In fact, the Socratic dialogue was a learning as well as a teaching process. Anaxagoras, a name that has bobbed up in recent literature, survives as an experimental and theoretical scientist because he was a teacher. Most scholars would toss in their sleep if they thought the new trails they had found would not be used. We would surely light fewer candles if we did not believe that they would illuminate the way for others.

But if transmission is important to the survival of knowledge, it is equally important for the discipline it imposes on those who seek knowledge. Edward Purcell, the Nobel Laureate, recently said that he had learned more about physics working on the new physics course for secondary schools than in any equivalent three-month period in his life. Most teachers have found that explanation is necessary for the academic soul, and most teachers have also found that the process of explanation frequently proves that mental slips are showing. Many times we listen to ourselves with a critical second ear, knowing our lecture is full of holes, both in fact and logic. When we are not called to account, our relief is always tinged with disappointment that our audience was caught napping.

With regard to the third characteristic of knowledge—its application or its use to man—much nonsense has been written about the difference between the proof of knowledge and the utility of knowledge. Certainly proof and utility are different ideas and involve different values. But just as certainly, proof without concern for the application of proof leads straight to the barren discussions of medieval scholasticism, while proof based on utility alone makes generalization impossible and thus leads to the destruction of knowledge itself. The two ideas of proof and utility are different but dependent, and their interaction lies at the very center of the enlightenment and progress of mankind. "This intimate union of theory and practice aids both," says Whitehead. "The intellect does not work well in a vacuum."

I have dwelt on the close connections of acquisition, transmission, and application of knowledge at some length because we cannot understand the modern university unless we understand these three aspects of knowledge. This is so because the three aspects of knowledge have their institutional reflections in the three missions of the university: the acquisition of knowledge is the mission of research; the transmission of knowledge is the mission of teaching; and the application of knowledge is the mission of public service.

It could be expected to follow that the three missions of the university are as organically related as are the three aspects of knowledge. I most profoundly believe that this is so. I also believe that these three missions not only describe the functions of the modern university—they also provide it with its enormous powers and its enormous problems.

But before we are ready to grapple more intimately with powers and problems, let us place the three great missions of the university in historical perspective. Perhaps this will help to illuminate the unique nature of the institution as we know it in modern America.

It is important to note that the three aspects of knowledge have not always been given equal emphasis. On the contrary, one aspect or another has customarily been emphasized throughout history at the expense of the other two. And this emphasis has largely been determined, at any given time, by the level of intellectual sophistication and the nature of the social environment that prevailed. Traditional societies were and are, naturally enough, bound to be preoccupied with traditional knowledge, and that kind of knowledge is a weak elixir for the rejuvenation of that kind of society. For such a society, the idea of university-based research is almost meaningless, possibly irrelevant, and certainly dangerous.

Thus the concern for knowledge was for centuries restricted to a concern for what *was* rather than what *could be*—to a transmission of old knowledge rather than a search for the new. And at the center of the wheel of history was the fact that the rulers of traditional societies, both clerical and civil, were not hospitable to the idea that truth could be discovered without the intervention of those specially trained in the mysteries. The authoritarian structure of the Middle Ages had to be dissolved by the Renaissance, the Reformation, the rise of the middle classes, and the revolution of scientific technology before change could become a desirable goal rather than a danger to be avoided. When the traditional crust was broken and man's curiosity and aspirations could assert themselves, the search for new knowledge was on. The universities became ready to produce it, and society prepared itself to receive it and use it. But not immediately, and not everywhere.

The German universities, in the third decade of the nineteenth century, were the first to raise the banner of research as a central mission—if not the central mission—of the university. The combination of the industrial revolution in the cities and the nationalistic fervor among the intellectual classes brought new intellectual life to the German university. Within two decades this combination had transformed both the theory and the practice of higher education.

But the flowering of the German university took place in a shady garden without appropriate drainage or fertilizer. The process was confined to an elite—around five per cent of the age group, at its maximum—and as a result the trained manpower needed to fuel German growth simply was not forthcoming. Even more important was the disjunction between the German university and German society, a disjunction that arose out of the monarchic, aristocratic, and essentially antidemocratic nature of the German ruling classes. The university could expect support as long as it did not meddle in affairs outside its walls. Conversely, there was little incentive for the research scholar to establish relations with public and private authorities. Thus the promotion of basic research became the true mission of the university, and both the university and German society were content.

But the price was high, both for higher education in Germany and for the social structure of the country. Neither its government nor its business leaders had the benefit of the humanizing influence that close contacts with the university might have provided. And the university was denied the stimulating feedback that would have come if it had been free to adapt both its academic doctrine and its organization to the requirements of a modernizing country. As a result, the missions of instruction and public service were neglected. The price of this neglect has been paid by each generation and is now a towering social and political problem for the managers of modern Germany.

In England the pattern was quite different. In Oxford and Cambridge, those two great bellwethers of English higher education, the resident undergraduate colleges were, and still are, the controlling elements. They have the money and the administrative muscle, so while collegiate functions could prosper, university interests were bound to be undernourished. Thus these two most ancient and most distinguished universities have become the measuring rods for excellence in undergraduate instruction.

But this decentralized and undergraduate-oriented environment was not very hospitable to research and graduate study, and even less so to interaction with English society. Without the continuous yeasty influence of new knowledge and the rude intrusion of new requirements, undergraduate education might be gracious but not necessarily stimulating; sometimes it may even be irrelevant. The promotion of research, advanced studies, and public enterprise— all of them university-wide responsibilities—has languished. Who was there to promote them against the collegiate inertia? A recent Cambridge University self-study reinforced this point when it stated: "The crux of any reorganization seems to us to be the provision of more personal direction of the University's affairs. A great University cannot work efficiently unless several senior men devote virtually the whole of their time to transforming policy decisions into action; bringing business to a head; reflecting on how one decision interacts with other decisions, negotiating both inside and outside the University; and doing a vast amount of informal consultation which cuts across committees."

These and similar considerations have produced a series of reports from Crowther, Robbins, and others; but real change will come hard. Until change comes at all, Great Britain will be without the benefit of that dynamo of the modern world—the modern university.

The moral is that the university in Germany and the university in England have both suffered because they have overemphasized one of the three missions, and the resulting biases are now frozen in the organizational concrete of the German institute and the English college. Now that German, and particularly English, social and economic development both demand and need a new and more rounded orientation in higher education, the universities face a major upheaval if they are to respond.

The two experiences testify further that the acquisition, transmission, and application of knowledge are organically connected. Institutional policies and arrangements that grossly neglect one function in favor of the others build a low ceiling indeed on the institution's future growth and vitality.

The third and relatively underdeveloped characteristic of knowledge—its application to the world supporting the university—was clearly foreshadowed by Franklin and Jefferson, those farsighted products of eighteenth-century enlightenment. Both were early champions of the university's responsibility to include practical studies for the new age then struggling in early adolescence.

They dreamed of an open society, free of both ecclesiastical and civil control, with little to fear from the uninhibited search for truth or from experiments in the application of truth. The idea that a university should be useful required a society that would put it to use. It was the great genius of Franklin and Jefferson that they saw both developments as interrelated and important.

But they were prophets ahead of their time. Universities in name remained colleges in fact. All of higher education was in the doldrums until the Civil War released the industrial energies that had been growing beneath the surface of an agricultural society. The grip of classical traditions was broken,

and the dreams of Jefferson and Franklin were en-
acted into law in the Morrill Land Grant Act of
1862.

And then everything began to blossom at once.
American universities became the heirs of the Brit-
ish tradition of undergraduate instruction and the
German concern for graduate education and
research, and joined both to the new mission to be
"in the nation's service." For the first time in history,
the three aspects of knowledge were reflected in the
three modern missions of the university. The results
were both revolutionary and explosive. They
changed the whole relationship between the university and society. And in the process, they produced a new idea of the university.

The first area to feel the impact of the new idea
of the university was agriculture—not unnaturally,
since the need to apply technology to agriculture
was one of the driving requirements behind the
Land Grant Act. From this concern for agricultural
technology emerged the powerful partnership including the private sector, the government, and the university. Here the university combined with county,
state, and federal agencies and private associations
to produce a unique transmission belt by which
ideas for the application of technology to the production and distribution of food could be translated
into action. The same groups have worked out a

balance of relationships that have led to the rapid reduction of farm workers and farmed land while food production has soared. It is reasonably safe to say that modern industrial development is almost impossible unless the farming population can be reduced and those freed from the farm made available for industrial and service industries. Today less than eight per cent of the working population is involved in the production of food. But this eight per cent produces more food and better food than did four times its number just a few generations ago.

The cyclical processes continue unabated. Research continues to pour from our universities and is rapidly translated into hardier grains, healthier animals, and more scientifically oriented farmers. And these farmers and their agents present the universities with ever new requirements for new ideas. This dynamic revolution has surely resulted from the functioning of the three related missions of the university—a process which has transformed the agricultural community and is operating at an ever-increased tempo. As the number of farmers and farms decrease, the pressure to apply more and more advanced technology continues to mount. The miraculous results of this whole process may be the only hope for millions of hungry persons in the world.

Of course, this dynamic interchange has not been

confined to agriculture. In lesser or greater degree, it can be found in other fields of knowledge and in areas of public need. Engineering education was to industry what agricultural education was to the farm. And scientific research was behind both. Studies in public administration have introduced new criteria of excellence into the management of public business, which in turn has increased the demands on schools (like this great one at Princeton). As these demands are met with new ideas and better trained graduates, government sights will be further raised to produce new requirements for the School of Public and International Affairs.

The worlds of literature and the arts have also felt the invigorating effect of an interchange between the scholar and the writer, the musicologist and the musician, and the school of drama and the theater. Indeed, this interchange has proceeded to the point where there is now a most interesting debate in progress as to the proper role of the university in the arts.

Thus, there is practically no field that has not grown and prospered from the dynamic interrelations that now exist within the university, on the one hand, and between the university and public and private agencies on the other. The university and the other institutions of society—including the corporation, the farm, the cultural center, and the

government agency—have now been joined together
by a new kind of blood stream, made up of the
ideas, the trained intelligence, and the manpower
which provide the driving energy for our society.
And the university is the great pumping heart
that keeps this system fresh, invigorated, and in
motion.

As this stream has run from the university to the
corporation and the government bureau and back
again, it has transformed both government and industry: the ideas and manpower of the university
have helped turn government to an increasing pre-
occupation with public welfare, and they have
helped give the profit-making corporation a far
larger public orientation than it has ever had before.
We should note again that this mixture of private
pursuit and public purpose is hardly conceivable
without the universities as partners, and this partnership would be impotent if the university had not
come to embrace its complementary missions which
have enabled it to digest new ideas, train new students, and participate in new applications.

The interplay of forces that the modern university has thus triggered has transformed our whole
society—and the university with it. Our university
is the engine of change and is transformed by it.
For this story of success is also a story of the dangers

of success: the functions of the university must now be performed amid the pressures of exceedingly rapid growth. Let us see what this has meant.

The first and most obvious manifestation of this growth has been the enormously increased load on instruction—an increase which has been both quantitative and qualitative. The college-age population has steadily risen, with a noticeably large jump after World War II for reasons that would be described by the building experts as deferred maintenance. At the same time, the percentage of those who wish to enter the university has expanded even faster. These two factors, powerful enough by themselves, have been joined by a third—a social philosophy which suggests that everyone should go beyond secondary education if he wishes, and should be financed if he hasn't the funds. As a result, we have almost five and one-half million students in our system of higher education each year, and we are adding four hundred thousand more—the equivalent of almost one hundred new Princetons—annually!

On the qualitative side, secondary education has improved dramatically, particularly since our rude awakening by Sputnik in 1957. As a result, the responsibilities for general education have slowly been assumed by the high school and the preparatory school. In the university, general instruction has given way to far more sophisticated work in the first two years. When the change in content and method has been too slow, the very good student has joined the ranks of the discontented. We shall deal with some of the reasons for student discontent more fully later.

Both pressures have come at a time when the pool of faculty talent has been reduced by the low birth rates of the depression and when that pool has also been tapped for the skills and talents needed by government, industry, and a variety of important services. Small wonder that undergraduate education has suffered in the university.

Meanwhile, scholarship and research, both basic and applied, have come to feel the great internal pressures of unleashed curiosity and the external demands of national interest. Periods of dramatic change stimulate the minds of everyone, and the pulse of this interest can be felt by scholars in every field of knowledge. Just list the summer activities of any faculty, and you will be astonished to discover that its members have scattered to the corners of the earth—not to escape, but to learn. And on their return, like bees from honey flights, the entire university hive is the beneficiary.

Still another factor adding to the university's growth has been the rising national interest in university research, strongly backed by federal dollars. The impact of all this on the university has been well documented by the Carnegie and Brookings studies and has been vividly described by Clark Kerr under the heading, "The Federal Grant University."

The results of this federal interest, I might add, have been soundly flailed in recent months by almost every critic in search of a subject. The problems created for the university are real enough. Instruction has frequently taken second priority; buildings, even when paid for by the government, involve increased operating costs; overhead returns are rarely adequate; and most colleges of arts and sciences feel, with some justice, that government rewards to the sciences tend to widen still further the breach between C. P. Snow's two worlds.

But the positive benefits of federal involvement cannot be ignored. The stimulation of scientific effort has brought new standards of excellence and new dimensions of service to most universities. Without any question, the natural sciences and engineering have made quantum jumps in their sophistication, and their fields are some of the most exciting in the curriculum. Moreover, federal support is now broadening to include the social sciences, and the new Humanities Foundation will include the arts. So universities will continue to receive the country's attention and the country's support.

Finally, the pressures of external demand have been felt directly by university staffs themselves. Once at work on a project initiated and often largely financed from the outside, faculty members find it an easy step to move from the university into government bureaus and industrial establishments, some to proffer their advice and counsel, others often to stay for good. But wherever their activities lead them, the involvement of faculty members in specific projects with outside agencies is likely to do two things: first, to bring more new projects to the university; and, second, to lead to increasingly complex, if not disorderly, administrative relationships both within the university itself and between the university and other agencies.

Meanwhile, the spiral continues. Growth begets more growth, and specialization more specialization. Discovery leads only to more questions, which require new ideas and more specialized training, which—in turn—produce more discoveries. As the relations between the university and other institutions of society proliferate, it will become a major task of the universities to draw the lines between their legitimate and illegitimate functions and to see clearly where their mission begins and ends. No wonder that the despairing trustee and administrator have frequently shared the longing of the bewildered student and critic for a return to some academic Walden.

But the pressures and demands will continue from the outside, too. More and more young people will want the education that opens doors to the good life; there will be more and more problems to be attacked—moral, aesthetic, scientific, economic, social, and political; and there will be more and more demands for an imaginative application of knowledge around the world. The university—as the most sophisticated and, let us hope, independent agency now at work advancing, transmitting, and applying knowledge—has come too far to retreat before what may be its finest hour.

Yet the crucial questions remain: What will be the effects of this vast growth? In what direction is the university heading? Perhaps even more to the point, can the university keep pace with the modern world, let alone bear the torch that lights the way?

We may be able to respond to these questions by the end of these lectures. But there can be no denying the deep concern of all those who see the future as an extension of the recent past. Already too large in many cases, how can our universities absorb twice as many students in the next decade? Already extended by the demands and excitement of research, how can they survive the inevitably increased demands that come from the dynamic interchange we have just described? Already under pressure for services that take the university to every corner of the earth, how can they reply to the insistent demands of the new nations?

Various experts have predicted the future of the university by making projections of the recent past. The results are frightening. They are also not necessarily reliable. But they can stimulate us by picturing a future we must do our best to avoid.

The first of these projections was made famous by George Beadle, President of the University of Chicago. It is called the Brontosaurus projection, and it suggests that growth is out of hand. With a body growth curve far exceeding a mind growth curve, the university is doomed to repeat the sad history of the prehistoric monsters which are presumed to have emitted great noise but few constructive comments.

Then there is the Caretaker's Daughter projection. You will remember the old song that runs something like, "Who takes care of the caretaker's daughter when the caretaker's busy taking care?" With faculty in orbit, students out looking for their lost identities, and administrators out setting off dynamite under foundation vaults—who is taking care? Who says no to large-scale research enterprises? And on what theory? Who is in charge?

Next there is the Kent projection. This projection

receives its title from a lady in Kent made famous in a limerick generally attributed to Don K. Price (and made still more famous by Clark Kerr):

> There was a young lady from Kent
> Who said that she knew what it meant
> When men took her to dine
> Gave her cocktails and wine
> She knew what it meant—but she went.

The Kent projection suggests that the university will become increasingly an agent rather than a principal—an agent whose facilities are available and whose activities will be determined more and more by the requirements of the state. In this image, the university would become an institution always for hire, and increasingly for hire for the short-run rather than for the long-run needs of society.

Finally, there is Kerr's Constructive Chaos projection. Here the arresting point is made that institutional integrity may be a danger rather than an asset. It may stifle creativity rather than protect it. It can limit freedom as well as extol it. It can be parochial, inward looking, reflective on past glories rather than preoccupied with the future. It can be resistant to change in the name of preserving institutional balance.

Therefore, the Kerr theory holds that university

response to government blandishment for scientific research is a good thing—it has brought progress through constructive imbalance. Administrative neutrality has brought academic freedom through independence and mobility. And institutional decision-making decentralized down to the individual professor has made change possible with the fewest university convulsions. In short, institutional administrative integrity may be too high a price to pay if it comes at the expense of change and the restlessness that rapid change requires.

From our four projections we can find the four most common fears about the future of the university. The fear of uncontrolled growth—the Brontosaurus projection. The fear of loss of direction—the Caretaker's Daughter projection. The fear of loss of principle—the Lady from Kent. And finally, the fear that the university will be too rigid in an era of rapid change.

In fact, they boil down to two primary concerns. The first has to do with the external relations of the university—that it may lose its identity. The second has to do with the internal cohesion of the university—that it may lose its capacity to manage its own affairs. And since these two concerns reflect the deepest fears and deepest aspirations of mankind, we may well believe we are at the heart of the fears and aspirations of mankind's great intellectual institution.

So we shall continue our discourse next by an examination of the internal problem, and then we shall look at the external problem. We may even discover how these two concerns connect.

II

THE SEARCH
FOR
INTERNAL
COHERENCE

II

THE SEARCH

FOR

INTERNAL

COHERENCE

WE HAVE DISCUSSED the attributes of knowledge—its acquisition, transmission, and application—and discovered that they correspond to the three missions of the modern university: teaching, research, and public service. We suggested that the explosive power of knowledge might be traceable to an interaction of its attributes, and that in like manner the growth and current power of the university in the United States might derive from the fact that it, and perhaps it alone, had fully embraced its three missions.

We also observed that, in the midst of all this, the modern university appears threatened by its own success. There are some indications that the university may, in responding to society's urgent demands that it enlarge its research, teaching, and service functions, risk the fate which size and mindlessness imposed on the dinosaurs. It is a chilling thought, but I have hinted at my optimistic belief that we can avoid such a fate by the exercise of our reason and our organizing abilities.

We shall deal here with some of the more formidable problems which the university faces internally, within its own family on campus. Many of these problems have been created by the growth of the institution and also by the vast attending explosion in knowledge itself. Many of them are wrapped up, too, in the constant debate about the university's integrity, and that may be, therefore, a good place to start.

It is popular these days to talk about the compromising of university integrity, and to decry, in the words of one critic, the weakening of the university's "capacity to fulfill its function as the corporate agent of free inquiry." Presumably, integrity is something good the university once had and is now losing with every response to the forces that would change the *status quo* or compromise intellectual chastity with new social involvement.

I think we must be very careful that we do not turn integrity into a "dry-ice" word which freezes everything it touches. Certainly, it cannot be used to solidify the *status quo* and to resist change, for change has long been the watchword of university development, and adaptation the key not only to its survival but to its enormous vitality and usefulness. Those who promulgated the Yale report of 1828 doubtless believed that to introduce engineering into the course of studies was to violate the university's integrity. If so, they were confusing the university's purposes with its traditions. Similarly, the addition of a law school to Princeton would surely not affect its integrity, whatever it might do to its traditions and its style.

University integrity, then, is involved not with preserving things as they are, but rather with maintaining the coherence of its various parts, and the harmony with which it is able to pursue its aims— whatever their specialized nature. Are the university's pursuits carried out to assure work of the highest order, with thoroughly professional standards and with clarity of purpose? Even more important, are the university's efforts in research, instruction, and public service undertaken in such a manner that each mission supports the other? We have already noted that these three missions are subtly and intricately meshed. It follows that the real integrity of the university is violated when large decisions in one area do not consider the impact on the other two. I would state it even more strongly: university integrity is compromised when decisions about any one of our three aspects of university activity fail to *strengthen* the others.

Keeping in mind these considerations which should influence the university's response to pressures for growth and change, let us look now at some of the factors which can help to inhibit the uncontrolled growth of the university—and which, to that end, can work in our favor.

With respect to research, the controlling factor is the increasing necessity for choosing among fields and areas where the university can expect to excel. Knowledge is growing so fast that no university can pretend to cover it all—at least not with any hope of maintaining high professional standards. Even a single department of physics or philosophy must decide to concentrate within its respective field. Uncontrolled growth may come, therefore, from an uncontrolled selection of areas for excellence and it follows that the university can and must choose among possibilities. The very nature of the knowledge explosion and the desire for highest standards will force choice and thus will act as a brake on uncontrolled growth.

It is wrong to say that this choice must not be influenced by outside considerations. On the contrary, there may be a pressing public need which attracts a university's attention, or an opportunity to draw superior talent to the campus, perhaps even combined with the availability of funds. Let me add quickly that the funds alone cannot be the determinant. But their availability may insure the highest standards for the activity to be financed—if it is the right activity. Whether it be in high-energy physics or comparative linguistics, if the activity fits into the university scene, the presence of funds should not be a barrier to the addition, nor its acceptance a violation of integrity. It is the casual, unreflective, opportunistic development of interests for the sole purpose of attracting funds and prestige which obviously violates integrity.

While research must operate under the restraints of choice and excellence in the disciplines, instruction must operate under the restraints of student numbers and student selection.

We must remember that the most important factor in the pressure for university growth is the increased percentage of the age group that is demanding access to higher education. The figure is now well on its way to 50 per cent. But there is a great difference of opinion as to what the trends may be in the future. Some believe 50 per cent will represent something of a plateau. Others believe that there may actually be an accelerated increase after that figure is reached as more young people move out of a minority status.

If those who predict a relatively slow growth are

correct, the pressure from increasing numbers will begin to lose some of its steam in the foreseeable future. Then the system as a whole will be relieved, though the prestige universities will hardly feel it. As the Negro spiritual puts it, "No resting place down there." Such universities may find restrictions on further growth arising from student reaction to an overcrowded campus. As more colleges and universities achieve higher standards, there may well be a disposition to pass up those whose size is, from the social or even intellectual point of view, forbidding. There are already signs of such a development, aided and abetted by avowed government policy to promote geographic equality. But, alas, neither Cornell nor Princeton is large enough to be very much benefited by this prospective development either.

More important than any prospective leveling-off of enrollments, however, is the rapid emergence of alternatives to the university, primarily in private and state-supported systems of junior and four-year colleges. Certainly the absence of enough satisfactory alternatives has been responsible for some of the excessive enrollments in our universities—though we have not suffered anything like the growth of such institutions as the University of Mexico, with over 80,000 enrolled students, or Buenos Aires, with over 60,000, both of which are operating in systems where there are no alternatives at all. Now in the United

States there are many alternatives—the junior and four-year colleges; courses given through educational TV, with off-campus testing programs; and various types of correspondence, radio, and taped curricula—all of which are beginning to drain off some of the demand for university attendance. Obviously, the universities have a profound stake in the successful development of these alternative measures, and for this reason they should lend their weight and prestige to assure that these measures are successful. Their own preservation will be at stake.

In its public service undertakings, the university may also find some natural restraints working to limit growth, although it is true that the demands of our fast-growing technological society are voracious and are becoming more so along the whole growing edge of social change: there is almost no problem in our society that does not increasingly require expert advice. It is also true that expert advice can be found most frequently and in greater variety in the university than in any other institution; indeed, hardly any field of knowledge in the university has not felt the heady experience of being publicly useful.

But the unique contribution of the university in all of this is knowledge, not operating skills, and this should be a limiting factor of great importance.

The government and particularly the corporation have been organized in our society to get things done, and it is to these institutions that society normally looks for operational responsibility. The university social scientists can provide the economic case for a state sales tax, for example, but they should not be expected to collect the money. It is legitimate for a university engineer to design a bridge, but not to involve the university in building it. And it is often to the university's credit that its agronomists are called upon to discuss the corn-hog price ratio, but it makes no sense for the university to participate in the mechanics of that complicated business. The fact that lines can be and are drawn between advice on how to do something and assistance in doing it thus constitutes a limiting force which aids the university in its need to preserve its balance and its unity.

Turning from these factors which may impose certain general restrictions on the growth of university missions, we face a whole range of internal decision-making which affects the size and shape as well as the direction of the institution. I have already suggested that the essential criteria to guide this internal decision-making grow from the interrelatedness of the university's missions, and that the university's capability in each area must be strengthened by decisions regarding the other two. Let us see how this is so, by examining the ways in which each mission of the university must be specifically related to the others—if integrity is to be preserved.

Few would contest the proposition that research and instruction are intimately connected. Volumes have been written supporting the proposition that university-level instruction can best be accomplished by faculty members who themselves are working at the frontiers of knowledge. The teacher-researcher is the ideal. The argument is rarely over any conflict between the functions; it most generally involves questions of degree and emphasis.

But the university gives too little attention to those courses of instruction that mesh with the university's research responsibilities. If we wish the ideal professor to teach and undertake research at the same time, then it must follow that the nature of the teaching and the research must be conditioned by the fact that they are to be carried on by the same person. If the teaching and the research are not in some way coordinated, we will have faculty members who are attempting to lead coherent lives while their research is headed in one direction and their teaching in another.

Unfortunately, this is precisely what happens in most universities. The undergraduate curriculum, particularly in the first two years, is based on the familiar doctrine of general education. This theory holds that the student, irrespective of his future specialty, should be exposed early to a common body of knowledge—at the least, to an introductory course in each of the divisions of the humanities, the social sciences, and the natural or biological sciences. The emphasis is cultural and general—a preparation for life rather than a preparation for a profession or a career.

But for the faculty member, research is particular and special, and the man really living at the edge of knowledge will frequently find that participation in survey or introductory courses requires an abrupt change of gears. Small wonder that instruction for the first two years finds relatively few of the greatest scholars either willing or able to make the necessary adjustments. Introductory courses for future majors will sometimes attract them from their research lairs, but a room full of freshmen ready to fulfill a distribution requirement can be a forbidding prospect. Pressure to perform will only encourage acceptance of the next offer from a more sympathetic institution.

There have been two main answers to this problem. The first has been to separate the graduate and the undergraduate faculties. This resolves, in part, the problem of intellectual schizophrenia; no professor is expected to perform at two different levels at the same time. But the price is separation within the university—an undergraduate college whose faculty members suffer from the suspicion that they are second-class or, at best, that they are involved in a university activity at the second level of importance.

The other answer has been to maintain the single faculty, but to divide it by age—the novices for teaching and the established professors for research. Of course, the final solution must involve some compromise of these extreme positions, because there are many famous full professors who bend their backs to contribute to the improvement of undergraduate instruction. In many cases the problem is resolved by a discreet distribution of teaching loads within departments, based upon tacit assumptions of the teaching and research capabilities of individual faculty members. Sometimes there is an equally subtle distribution of teaching responsibilities among departments. History and government faculty, for example, have traditionally carried a heavier load of teaching hours than anthropology and sociology professors, because the behavioral wing of the social sciences is more scientifically oriented and less digestible by students in pursuit of a general education.

The problem at best is a very difficult one, but we have enormously complicated its solution by acting as if undergraduate education in a university can be the same thing as undergraduate education in a four-year liberal arts college. We suffer, I suggest, from the fallacy buried in the assumption that the first two years of higher education should be the same in all institutions, be they independent colleges or universities. We also suffer from the even more profound fallacy that all students who enter the liberal arts college or the university have the same educational needs and motivations.

These two broadly held and fallacious assumptions are at the heart of the strain between instruction and research at our universities. Those who hold them insist on a generality of studies that serves only to drive out of the lecture halls many faculty who are committed to research. We have often assumed that where teaching and research do not mesh, the research faculty should be punished and the teaching faculty rewarded. Special inducements for teaching may well be necessary, and they may help reduce the problem. But the means are artificial.

The fact is that undergraduate instruction and admissions policies need modification in order to assure the internal coherence and integrity of the university through a closer coordination of the teaching and research functions. I shall not lay out a blueprint here, but some general observations are in order.

First, I think we must break the lock step that would keep all institutions and students working in the same patterns and at the same pace. We must be prepared to recognize that undergraduate instruction can and must be different in a university than it is in a college, for example, and that it can and must appeal to a special category of student. The trend to design different programs to fit different institutions and different students has already begun; we must accelerate it.

Second, we shall have to hold tight to the ideals of a liberal education but recognize that, in the face of rapidly improving secondary education and the multi-concerns of the modern university, the style of liberal education will have to be adapted to its environment.

We might all agree that the threefold purpose of liberal education is to learn to know nature, society, and ourselves; to acquire certain skills, such as clear expression and a grasp of the scientific method and discipline; and finally, to embrace certain values, such as intellectual honesty, tolerance, and the capacity for wise judgment.

But the curriculum and the system for assuring a liberal as well as a professional education must surely take into consideration the missions of the university. This will mean, among other things, a reexamination of the idea that general education is something that is sandwiched between secondary-school and upper-class work. Rather than occupy two or more years of pre-professional study, liberal education may have to run on a track parallel with professional work. For the student who wants to specialize, therefore, liberal education will have to be provided either by the secondary school or by a special program that includes liberal along with professional studies—or a combination of both. After all, a liberal education is the objective of a lifetime. Why assume it should be crowded into the first two post-secondary years?

The improvement of liberal education in the university will also require attention to the way subject matter is presented. There can be a liberal and a professional way of treating any subject. In a university it becomes particularly important that the research-oriented professors have as broad a view of their subject as possible. Just as instruction will have to be adapted to interest the professor, so will the professor have to teach his subject in a liberal style to interest the student.

Third, the flexibility and independence of graduate-level work will have to characterize a larger proportion of undergraduate education, too. This is already beginning to happen in the upper-class years; it may have to be extended down into the first two years for those students who are ready for it—and there are many more than we think. Honors work and educational experimentation can also help lighten the heavy dough of our undergraduate course programs. Whatever solutions we provide, we will have to give our fullest attention to improving our programs for our best students if they are not to be lost in the crowd.

Finally, we must know a great deal more about the kind of preparation, maturity, and motivation that should determine the selection of students for university-level work. Those who need the sense of security that comes from being a member of a smaller, tighter community should not come to the university. For when they do, they keep looking for a kind of faculty-student relationship that can best be found in an independent liberal arts college, a fruitless search that adds to the problem of internal cohesion in the university.

The application of these criteria might drastically modify the number of undergraduates who would come to the university as opposed to the college. Such criteria would surely affect the whole tone and purpose of the university, and they would make possible the reintroduction of the undergraduate to the research professor. But most of all, they would tend to bring teaching and research together and so help make our university communities coherent again.

Let us examine next the relations between the transmission and application of knowledge—between instruction and public service. Too frequently, I am afraid, we view the intellectual development of the student, to paraphrase Alfred North Whitehead, as if he had neither a body nor a soul. But even when we don't, we consign his physical and spiritual requirements to the area of extracurricular activities— a term frequently conjured up to secure the intellectual purity of the classroom.

Still, the student needs some connection between his studies and his concerns, between what he reads and what he sees, between what he thinks and what he does. This is complicated, because university-level study should require long periods of solitary study and reflection.

But the underclassman is not yet a library or laboratory scholar and must not be treated as one. Otherwise he will seek outlets for his concerns without the benefit of the moderating influence of his studies upon his actions. The head of the student government can discover to his lasting benefit that his experiences in campus affairs and his studies of public administration have some relation to each other. The same is true of the sociology student just returned from the South.

We have not been very inventive about how to relate studies and experience or thought and action, and the result can be frustration, or apathy, or even revulsion on the part of good students. There is an excitement and an important feedback that comes from actually seeing and experiencing the relevance of intellectual exercises.

Unquestionably, the notion that knowledge can and should be pursued for its own sake is at the heart of our lack of interest in connecting studies and concerns. We pay the price in student disinterest and in the proliferation of activities which do not have the discipline of intellectual content. A closer coordination of the student's two lives would bring the university into better focus, and it would serve to aid the development of appropriate extracurricular activities, as well as add an important stimulus to intellectual growth. If there be doubters, I suggest they talk with a professor who has just seen his first book on publication day, or an anthropologist who has just returned from working with the Andean Indians, or an astrophysicist who has just seen his theories confirmed by recent descriptions of the moon's surface. The excitement of these men will be a reminder that the connection between thought and action, or between theory and results, which is so important to adults on the faculty, is even more important to students in the university.

In a larger sense, the ultimate use or application of knowledge must be brought under the restraints of research and instruction or the university is likely, in my view, to become unhinged. The pressing requirements of government and industry are, for the faculty member, full of the heady aroma of larger public purpose or prospective private gain. Both sensations are pleasant to an academic fraternity which for decades has been caricatured as impractical and which believes, with good reason, that it has been financially starved. In these circumstances, it is not surprising that faculty have taken to consulting with zest.

Again, we need criteria that will be useful in determining the directions and the merits of extra-university activity, and these criteria are to be found in our model of the three interconnected missions of the university. We must refer to the other two missions if we are to make valid decisions about the university's outside involvements. How can these strengthen the research and teaching functions?

Let me promptly remove from the discussion those matters which occupy the faculty in their capacities as private citizens. Everyone owes a part of his life to his society for public service, whether or not this service is directly connected with his profession. For those with a trained intelligence, such calls will not be lacking: they will increase as expert and disinterested service for the general welfare is in greater and greater demand.

But the outside activity which has a professional connection should, in general, have some feedback or use to the research interests of the professor and to the students who are dependent on him. Otherwise, the professor is just in business, or moonlighting, and his students are being shortchanged. Activities that are simply training projects, or are merely involved in implementing established knowledge and are not answering questions, should fall outside the boundaries of acceptable public activities for the university faculty.

The integrity of the university involves, then, a resistance to overexpansion of any of its three institutional functions, and the accompanying requirement that each institution will select its fields of specialization. Integrity involves, perhaps even more importantly, an insistence that all of the university's activities advance its capabilities to pursue each of its missions—that, as Whitehead has said, "all its various parts are coordinated and play into each other's hands."

This is a fine prescription, but it is idle to lay it down without talking about how it is to be achieved. Who is going to "manage" integrity? Who will select and control the complex and tightly interrelated tasks to be undertaken by the university? Who is to make the critical decisions that will prevent each phase of activity from growing out of balance and stifling the others? Who is to make the university and its missions a coherent whole?

It is clear, at the outset, that the answers will not

be precise or unequivocal. The university is not an orderly structure that yields to authoritarian management as does the military division or the corporation. The university's function is to serve the private processes of faculty and students, on the one hand, and the large public interests of society on the other. In this sense, it has no balance sheet of its own, no single product that can be annually measured, no performance tables for judging success. Even when seniors do well on admission to graduate school, there is always the haunting suspicion that success may be due more to the skill of the admissions committee than to the performance of the students.

Three groups participate in university management—the students, the faculty, and the administration. Let us talk about the student first. The undergraduate is generally on the campus no more than four years, a fact that tends to put the leadership of student movements in other countries more often than not in the hands of graduate students, and sometimes in the hands of those who make careers of student activities. The most vigorous student activities in the developing nations are led by students who have been enrolled for ten years and work full time at the business. But in this country, it is difficult to be a student and not attend classes sometimes. Furthermore, the prospects of a career are so bright that most students don't wish to delay their departures. Hence, management of the university is generally only on the edge of student interest.

In any case, management is not just a matter of deciding what would be good to do. Most importantly, it involves what is timely and what is possible. It involves what is wise. And wisdom requires, among other things, an understanding of the spirit of a particular institution, the interests of its campus leaders, its financial prospects, and the priorities it gives to various academic ventures. There is no substitute for careful observation of people and events over time. This kind of experience is denied the young, and it is an almost fatal disability for constructive participation in most university decisions.

Finally, the student is a student. He is at the university to learn, not to manage; to reflect, not to decide; to observe, not to coerce. The process of learning, like the process of research, is in the end a most private affair, requiring for the most part detachment and not engagement. If we learn to involve the student more highly in the formal learning process, we may even further reduce his desire for management.

But there are two comments that must be made on the other side of the argument. Some students will become strongly interested in university affairs. The student body will always include some with talents as administrators or leaders. These young people gravitate naturally into student government or the campus newspaper, seeking outlets for their interests. Their participation in university institutional activities is important for them because the university machinery is an immediate outlet for their organizational proclivities. It is also good for the university, which, at least as much as any other organization, is most likely to be improved by the ideas and the enthusiasms of imaginative, energetic young people.

There are, in connection with all of this, powerful forces at work that are raising the political temperature of the student and increasing his interest in university affairs. He is the product of an age of earlier freedom and later responsibility. Left on his own as a teenager, he is coming to the university and finding that the faculty is as peripatetic as his parents. He encounters a vacuum at the point of his greatest need—wisdom and advice on how to become an adult. He also finds a community which frequently seems not much interested in his education. He may well be mistaken in many cases, but he does feel an impersonality about the campus and a concentration on matters that involve him only tangentially. For many the answer is access to the machinery of the university—they want to reorder its priorities in their favor.

It would be foolish to deny the elements of justice

in this line of reasoning. It would be equally foolish to refuse to listen to those who wish to be heard. We welcome them as freshmen with speeches that tell them they are now adults, and so we must expect to treat them as adults.

There is another point to be made. Students do not like to be excluded, *in principle,* from the machinery of the university. Nor, indeed, does anyone else. A careful selection of places where student participation can be accepted because of known interest or known talent will most frequently be a stabilizing and integrating act rather than the contrary.

The disabilities of the students' short stay, inexperience, and scholarly preoccupations remain. But as long as students feel they have entered a place where there are no priorities, or where the priorities work against their real interests as students, the pressure for involvement will be strong and perhaps irresistible. Uncontrolled, this will ruin good scholars and good universities. Dealt with sympathetically, it will help bring about successful campus integration.

The faculty, as managers of the modern university, also offer certain limitations, arising from quite different circumstances. The community of masters was a noble and even feasible idea when there were only the four faculties of medicine, theology, law, and philosophy, and when the professor lectured several times a week and rarely saw students—as individuals—except in the corridors. The universities were in the big cities and the faculties were given appointments in the university but continued to participate in the main stream of city life. Outside the lectures there was precious little to administer in the university, so faculty decision-making was largely limited to appointments to the faculty itself. The nearest analogy would be to a modern departmental meeting, although the departmental meeting deals with academic affairs and logistical considerations in far more detail than did the whole university faculty of even a century ago.

But apart from size and complexity, the faculty as faculty has faced the additional difficulties we have noted in the enormous fractionalizing of the fields of knowledge, combined with an equally great increase in outside activities. The faculty has now become dispersed in several faculties, colleges, and departments; it has been divided into C. P. Snow's two worlds; and it has turned increasingly outward, away from the institution of the university, to the "guilds" that the scholars' special interests have led them to set up for themselves.

Partial views which are based upon increasingly specialized interests make it difficult for the faculty as faculty to have a point of view on broad institutional matters. Consequently, the faculty's administrative stance contains elements of senatorial courtesy —maximum permissiveness with respect to individual faculty desires, combined with maximum protection if anyone would interfere with this permissiveness. Such a posture is exactly right for the protection of the classroom, but it is quite inadequate for educational or institutional management.

So the university can never again run on the assumption that it commands or can command the full-time interest and attention of all its faculty. The nature of knowledge today is such that it requires minds and talents of quite a different order from those needed to make administrative decisions. And the faculty should be left as free as possible of administrative duties in order to do its work. As the interests of the disciplines and professions cut increasingly across institutional lines, faculty members must have access to the stimulation and fresh ideas that will certainly come from the interchange of outside meetings and conferences among specialists. The role of the university is to provide a framework and an environment where these ideas can be put to use—laboratories, libraries, classrooms, and studios —where creative work can be conceived, tested, explained, reformulated and tested again, and then sent out into the world.

But if faculty as a corporate body cannot be expected to manage the university, individual faculty members are indispensable to the management process. Indeed, I would put high on any university priority list the identification and support of those members of the faculty whose viewpoint is broad, who have that rare quality of seeing problems in operational terms, and whose faculty standing is solidly based on a specialized competence. They do not have to be drawn into full-time or even part-time administration. But they are the mainsprings of the university works, the heartbeat of its body, and the real initiators of reform and progress. Any university with a dozen such men as Mike Oates of Princeton and Max Black of Cornell can expect to grow and prosper; without them it will surely be bound in shallows and in miseries. Presidential leadership consists, in large part, of discovering these faculty leaders and then staying at their elbows, supporting their ideas, finding them money, guiding them when necessary, and encouraging them when the going seems rough.

Finally, there is the administrator, who is, in the end, charged with managing the integration of these many different and at times conflicting elements. The leadership of individual faculty members has brought new vigor to the university and will always be indispensable in accomplishing the particular tasks that interest them. And the faculty must always largely determine the shape and content of educational standards and educational policy.

But someone must be concerned with the institution as a whole, the activities it supports, the public face it presents, and the private concerns with which it is occupied. This job cannot be divided among disparate elements of the university. So it is the administrator—the president and others with managerial responsibility, cooperating with faculty and student leaders—who must be concerned both with the apparatus of the university and with the idea it represents. He must be able to involve himself directly in the central academic business of the university, to exert educational leadership, to be an agent for both stability and change. He must be capable of institutional justice and personal compassion. He must not fear power or be afraid to exercise it, because he must know that power cannot be the direct concern of either student or teacher. He must always be sensitive to the difference between the process of management and the process of education, and he must understand that the former must always serve the latter. Few large faculties have been able to provide this leadership for themselves. But without their general support, leadership cannot be effective.

It is this combination of institutional management and educational leadership that makes academic administration a unique and vital business. And it is this combination that is so necessary if any of the internal developments we have outlined are to have a chance to succeed.

The internal coherence of the university involves, then, attention to the missions of the university, their interdependence, and the optimum roles of student, teacher, and administrator in the management of this complicated task. It involves internal restraints in the pursuit of each mission, and the restraints that come from the necessity of considering the university missions as a coordinated whole. It involves clarity with respect to an educational philosophy that is appropriate to a university. It involves understanding of the respective roles and contributions of administration, faculty, and students to the internal management of the university.

In the center of this complicated community there are a group of students with strong administrative and educational instincts, a much larger group of faculty with strong institutional instincts, and a group of administrators sensitive to student values and aspirations and to faculty interests and attitudes. No university can function properly unless it has a balance of these groups who are preoccupied with its health and vitality. No university can develop in sensible ways unless a general consensus has been achieved at the heart of its institutional life among those concerned with its future. But it will be, I suggest, those who spend full time at the business of direction and management who must assure this consensus—who must see to it that educational purpose and institutional interests develop in harmony.

Even when the community has mastered the difficult task of internal self-government, the task of university direction, stability, and growth has not been stated in its full complexity. We have already said that the university is no longer a self-sufficient world: it has a central role in the drama of higher education in the world at large. The university must achieve not only an internal harmony, but a harmony that is in a state of constant adaptation to the outside world. It is to this matter of the evolving role of the university in the total structure of higher education that we must turn next.

III

FROM AUTONOMY
TO
SYSTEMS

FROM AUTONOMY
TO
SYSTEMS

WE HAVE TALKED about some of the internal aspects of the university in transition. We discussed the need for greater internal cohesion and coherence, and the means by which we might expect to obtain these highly desirable qualities. We closed on a note of hope. We also realized, I believe, that internal cohesion cannot now be complete simply because the university *is* in a state of transition. But we did identify some guideposts for educational doctrine and university management which might increase the prospects for university integrity and coherence.

The internal problem, however, is only one aspect of the university in transition. There is also a very substantial and complicated superstructure of educational interests and educational institutions that are being established outside of and over the univer-

sity; and if any extended comment on the university
is to be adequate, it must cover this emerging system
of which the university is simply a part. The fact
is that the university, which was conceived and has
long been thought of as a self-sufficient community
of scholars, now finds self-sufficiency a nostalgic
dream. Where the university has thought of itself
as an institution which could explore independently
the unity of knowledge, it now finds that it must
concentrate on specialized segments of knowledge
if it is to maintain excellence. Where the university
has admitted only reluctantly in the past that other
universities also exist—and then, let us face it,
mainly for the purpose of arranging football sched-
ules—universities now find that close collaboration
is a stark necessity. And finally, the university has
only recently begun to realize that important functions bearing on university life—such as testing, innovation, and planning—are increasingly organized
and managed from outside the university.

It is useful to note, in this regard, that the growth
of higher education has produced complexity, and
complexity has produced specialization, and specialization requires coordination, which means that new
institutions must be created to do the coordinating.
I have, on another occasion, referred to this law of
development and have made my bows to Caryl Has-
kins for putting the law in graphic terms. He spoke,

you will recall, of crystals, anthills, and universities as following the same general rule. I prefer the complex beauty of the crystal, but I know what he means about anthills.

Not only has the growth of higher education spawned a great number of colleges, institutes, and universities; it has also produced a great variety of them. So great is this variety that meetings of university presidents are frequently slowed down by the presentation that starts, "Now in my university, we do it differently." Pluralism is no textbook notion in higher education. (Just look at the list of such institutions in the state of New Jersey: there are public, private, large, small, coeducational, men's, women's, two-year, and four-year colleges and universities.) At the same time, this process of institutional specialization has led to a growing interdependence of the colleges and universities.

The explosion of knowledge, which is at the heart of modern university specialization, has been attended by another factor: the towering costs of our academic enterprises. The area study program requires more and more hard-to-get books and its personnel more and more airplane tickets; the physics lab requires an incredibly costly electron microscope; the college of agriculture requires an expensive computer to keep track of the health of the cattle in its region. No university could or should assume the expense of all these facilities itself. Moreover, the high level of expertise needed for all these enterprises is just not available on any single campus.

Again, the need for planning has given further impetus to extra-university authorities. With the rising clamor for admission to higher education, attended by an equal clamor for trained manpower, no political body at any level can afford to allow the public's great interest in educational development to be satisfied by mere chance. And the prospect of successful development would be minimal if it were to involve the close collaboration of wholly independent and autonomous units. Consider how competent Princeton and Rutgers in New Jersey or Cornell and Columbia in New York would feel to suggest large-scale educational plans for their respective states. They don't even think it is their job!

Now let us examine for a moment the emerging hierarchy of supra-university institutions. This entire new world is fascinating to behold—it is almost like watching islands rise out of the sea in response to subterranean upheavals.

It was natural that the first efforts at developing an American system of higher education would take place at the state level. Public higher education has always been essentially a state responsibility in America. Therefore, it was the governors and state legislators, with their political sensitivities, who felt the first hot demands for state plans and for institutions to carry them out. In the American tradition, the solutions have varied from one state to the next.

In California, the university itself is a coordinating unit, which embraces seven more or less autonomous campuses in one grouping. Four-year colleges make up another group, and junior colleges make up still a third. The private colleges and universities are the uneasy partners in this evolving state-wide system— proud of their independence but somewhat concerned about its consequences, wanting invitations to the party, but not sure that they want to dance.

In New York, the picture is very complex. The University of the State of New York is the legal umbrella under which all institutions, public or private, school or college, receive their charters and their accreditation. The Commissioner of Education is the president of this University, and his staff is its staff. The Regents of the University are appointed by the legislature. But higher education is under a separate and independent Board of Trustees appointed by the governor. Unlike the University of California, the State University of New York (not to be confused with the University of the State of New York) is responsible for all colleges and universities, both junior and senior, in the public domain. Private colleges and universities are also loosely linked with this enterprise—loosely, because they are frightened at the prospect of involvement, though they are at the same time determined to secure the maximum state assistance. This leads, you might correctly surmise, to a posture which some have been unkind enough to characterize as opportunism.

It is my impression that New Jersey is notable for having no state-wide system of higher education at all. To the outsider, Rutgers and its management are unsung heroes for having developed a great university in spite of, rather than because of, those who are responsible for the state's interest in education. The report of the Newsom Commission, on which it was my privilege to serve, might well receive further attention from those in high places. New Jersey cannot forever afford to appear near the bottom of the list of states with quality systems of higher education.

But even state-wide planning and state-wide administrative systems did not meet all the needs. The existence of comparable and expensive professional schools in adjacent states was found to be both inefficient and extravagant, particularly where dollars and staff were in short supply. In the interest of sharing resources, state governments and universities have banded together to form regional organizations based on interstate compacts.

From Autonomy to Systems

As we might expect, the region with the strongest sense of identity—the South—produced the first regional educational organization, the Southern Regional Education Board. It was soon followed by others: the New England Board of Higher Education and the Western Interstate Compact for Higher Education. These three organizations have become known affectionately in the trade as WICHE, NEBHE, and SREB. They cover 34 states and, through their very competent staffs, seek ways and means of assuring the highest quality of post-secondary public education with a minimum duplication of effort. It is now almost unthinkable that a major public university in any one of these three regions would start a large new professional school without having the matter discussed and evaluated by the regional organization.

All regional organizations are not of the state compact type and do not involve the direct participation of public authorities. In the Midwest, for example, the universities themselves have banded together to form the Committee on Institutional Cooperation of the Big Ten and the University of Chicago. In this case, the universities, not the state governments, took the initiative; even more uniquely, this Committee involves the equal participation of both public and private institutions. This type of organization strikes me as having some advantages over the state compact, most particularly because it encourages the public and private institutions to be partners rather than adversaries.

At the moment, the universities of Pennsylvania, New Jersey, and New York have the uncomfortable distinction of not being involved in any regional organization at all. It would be well for us to decide whether this is the result of indifference and neglect, or of great wisdom. My instinct, naturally enough, leans me to wisdom, but a nagging realism suggests that it might be indifference.

And then there is the Ivy League. Organized around intercollegiate athletics, it seems too bad that this group of distinguished universities has not always used its collective weight to support matters of educational importance. The Big Ten presidents now have agendas full of interesting educational ventures. I'm afraid we Ivy League presidents are often too much concerned with our independent national images to participate in such exercises. But perhaps I am wrong. I hope so.

Useful as organizations at the regional level are in the United States, they frequently suffer from being suspended between the two focal points of real political power—the state and the federal governments. Although the federal government has traditionally not had a direct responsibility for education, this situation is in the process of dramatic change. Perhaps predictably, this change has followed rather than preceded the development of a national interest in education. It has also followed the development of a national viewpoint on the part of educators. These factors, supported by a sharpened sense of national identity and purpose and a desire to see improved standards obtain everywhere in the country, have worked to form the early outlines of a national system of education, even though the process is still in its infancy. Let us look briefly at some of the present pieces of such a national system.

The first structures were, naturally enough, a series of associations of colleges and universities organized to exchange views about common problems. These associations have prospered and multiplied, and today they cover, on a national basis, every conceivable type and style of college and university. If there are any presidents or deans who feel they do not have access to these organizations, they are simply not reading their mail. Even within this welter of associations, the instinct for order has asserted itself with the formation of the American Council on Education as the top holding company for all the special groups, ranging from the American Alumni Council to the Association of American Colleges.

Then there are the great foundations with national and even international programs. Committed to spending their incomes wisely for new ventures, they must develop ideas of the national interest in education as guides to giving. And they do. But these ideas of the national interest, even though completely uncoordinated, serve to impress on the national community images of national purpose and national priorities that work their way into the plans and programs of public and private agencies. It is not just through their grants that the foundations exercise their influence, but also through the designs and strategies that determine their grants. Foundations serve, therefore, as national planners in the private educational sector, even though their plans are inchoate and unannounced, and even though the effects of these plans may not always be decisive.

Another segment of our national educational superstructure consists of the agencies which have been created to perform various functions that the universities could not perform individually and never got around to performing collectively. The need for a broadly based faculty retirement program, for example, which could make it possible for the professor to take his pension with him from one institution to the next, led to the creation of the Teachers Insurance and Annuity Association at the end of the first World War. Similarly, the need for a national program of testing for the admission of students to higher education led to the College Entrance Examination Board and the Educational Testing Service. The desire for national scholarship and fellowship programs, which would recognize the national distribution of talent, led to the Woodrow Wilson Fellowship Program and the National Merit Scholarship Corporation. And a mounting concern over the international aspects of higher education, including the development of higher education abroad, led to the formation of the Institute of International Education, the African-American Institute, and, more recently, Education and World Affairs.

Each of these organizations has been established to perform special tasks for higher education, but significantly, all of them have been organized at the instance of some source outside the university world. It is a somber thought that the universities have not had the imagination or the initiative to establish these agencies themselves. Meanwhile, these agencies are in rather awkward positions: they are under the supervision neither of the university nor of any other educational authority, except the *ad hoc* boards that were created to run them or the foundations that came up with the ideas and provided the original funds.

Activities of great importance to the universities are thus now completely outside their control. But it is well to note again that the system as a whole is still in transition. Sooner or later, either new concepts and structures will emerge which will embrace both the universities and these service organizations, or else the universities may decide to supervise the job themselves, as perhaps they should have all along.

In this connection, while universities have never been noted for their capacity to mount joint operations, one interesting new straw in the wind is the current effort to establish a national consortium of some 34 universities to build and manage a 200-billion-electronic-volt synchrotron. This development is the most interesting and the most promising of the many supra-university organizations created thus far. Of course, universities have combined to form consortia before—to run Brookhaven, for example, and to establish new universities in India. But this, to my knowledge, is the first one that is national in scope. Jerome Wiesner has observed that "the time has come to find a means by which the universities can accept more of the responsibility for the allocation and use of [federal] funds. I suspect," he added, "that neither the funding agencies, the universities, nor the individual researchers will welcome the suggestion."

Behind all these private organizations, of course, stands the brooding presence of the federal government—freshly committed to the improvement of educational opportunity, to the strengthening of institutions of secondary and higher education, to the encouragement of higher standards of performance, to the advancement of research required in the national interest, to an expansion of the creative arts, and to a concern for educational development in modernizing countries. An aroused government is thus responding on many fronts to a sharpened conception of the national interest in education.

But the role of government as coordinator and manager has yet to be brought into focus. Assistance comes from many government sources, and these sources are rising in status. Recently, Francis Keppel, former U.S. Commissioner of Education, was appointed to the level of Assistant Secretary for Education. Other signs and portents of an expanding federal interest are not hard to find. Questions of educational standards have already been raised by the government. Chicago has seen the federal government connect the idea of educational assistance to the even tougher idea of social justice. And vigorous federal attention is being given to problems ranging from the education of the disadvantaged and the quality of urban schools to medical education and the better distribution of university excellence throughout the country. This expanding federal role will put the most severe pressure on the public and private universities to evolve national organizations and programs of their own that will act as both counterparts and counterweights to the new federal interest.

Moving with a perspective even broader than that of the federal government, meanwhile, are those agencies busy with higher education at the international level. There are international regional bodies, such as the Union of Latin American Universities, the Council of Southeast Asia Universities, the new Council of African Universities, and the Carnegie-sponsored Council on Higher Education in the American Republics. And there are such universal bodies as the public UNESCO and the private International Association of Universities.

Although many of these groups are relatively recent—and some still quite fragile—they are beginning to monitor a variety of important studies that may well affect plans and planning at national, regional, state, and even university levels, particularly in the area of assistance to universities in the underdeveloped countries. As a sense of world community evolves, and increasingly it must, these international agencies will be in ever stronger positions to express their interests and to influence educational planning. I need not describe the delicate problems that will arise when local institutions must adapt their plans to international considerations, but I would note that the opportunities for heroic speeches which this will present to future university presidents are almost unlimited.

One can only hope that the professional quality of this summer's meeting of the International Association of Universities in Tokyo can set the tone and the pattern for future discussions among educators from diverse parts of the world. The evolution of world politics will, of course, have a decisive bearing on the prospects for development of international structures dealing with problems of higher education. In the meantime, we are to be encouraged that these groups are already beginning to form.

That is roughly the picture of the educational pyramid that is now emerging. Higher education is becoming a system that runs from the department through the college, the university, the state, the regional compact, the national association, and the international body.

Each of these organizations, arranged one on top of the other, represents a new interest at a new and larger geographical level. Cornell and Princeton have become part of a web of interest that stretches to UNESCO and the International Association of Universities.

The university is thus only one level in the whole vast hierarchy of education that has been built up around it. Below it are the department and the college—and the complex of liberal arts and technical schools—and above it are the state agencies, the regional organizations, the federal structures, and finally the international organizations.

Now, in the long run, this structure itself matters very little to society as a whole. What society cares about is not which level of this hierarchy has the right to lead and to make decisions. What ultimately matters is that the right decisions are made at the level most competent to make them, and that these decisions are carried out successfully. The approval of society will come, in the end, not by claims of privilege but rather from results observed over time. And the desired results will be in those areas where society asks the most of its educational system.

Let us look at several of the requirements that society imposes on education and examine the capabilities of the various levels to deal with them. For what we find here will give us an important clue to the distribution of power and—not least—to the crucial role of the university in the entire educational organization.

First, let us look at the protection of academic freedom, for without academic freedom there is no educational system worth discussing.

The department and the college within the university are important for organizing the defense of freedom; but since they do not have the legal authority to hire and fire, they obviously cannot do the job alone. The university faculty is even more important, first, because it can speak more easily for the university as a whole, and second, because it is the body that participates in setting the rules of tenure.

Important as the faculty is in the protection of academic freedom, however, clearly the real defense within the university comes from the joining of trustees, administration, and faculty. It is a simplistic and outdated notion that working together with trustees and administration results in compromise of academic freedom. As a matter of fact, in the overwhelming majority of cases, faculties, administrations, and trustees have developed a solid consensus on the subject of academic freedom, and scholars are well protected by it.

Beyond the university, concern for academic freedom attenuates as we move up the scale. It is not that regional and international bodies aren't interested; it is simply that they know they can't do anything about academic freedom, and they are concentrating on other matters. They assume that the universities are responsible for academic freedom and have the power to defend it.

We can conclude, therefore, that the unique combination of forces at the level of the university provides the greatest barrier to the violation of academic freedom. All other levels in the hierarchy, from the federal government to the department, would do well to conduct their affairs with this kept strictly in mind.

A second fundamental requirement posed for the educational system is the need for continuous change and innovation. This point hardly calls for detailed documentation at a time when the world is faced with vast needs for new ideas and for manpower trained in new areas of knowledge. Let us see how change is regarded at each level of the hierarchy we have just described.

Again, let us start with the department. A relatively flexible instrument when compared with the great professor in foreign universities who dominates his field, the department is in most cases essentially a conservative unit. Its actions and positions reflect its dominant elements and the forces that have been balanced to produce some kind of departmental consensus. Those who make the consensus are not likely to produce the revolution to upset it. Furthermore, departments are not easily subject to change from the outside. They have become specialized in their fields of knowledge to the point where faculty from other departments find it very difficult to recommend changes, even when they have a vague feeling that changes are in order. Professional specialization frequently cuts so deep that faculty in one specialty are not in the best position to see into the next academic channel. All of this makes change at the departmental level somewhat hard to come by.

At the level of the collegiate dean, innovation can be accomplished, but it is a delicate art. For the dean who wishes to exercise leadership, the task of innovation will be easier if he has arranged for the rotation of departmental chairmen. He can also wield great influence by concentrating his attention on filling the major vacancies with men of the highest professional quality and by keeping alert to those occasions when the time is ripe for improvement.

The same prescriptions apply to the university president, although, generally speaking, his access to funds gives him an even more powerful lever in effecting change. It is a lever, however, which he must employ with care, because he must not allow the availability of funds to become more important than the changes they are to effect.

While it is true that the president and dean must not be too vigorous in throwing their weight around, the role of university president as bashful educational leader is mostly nonsense and greatly overplayed. Presidential modesty may in the end be more a cloak for naïveté than a strategy for educational leadership. Of course, administrative arm-twisting in support of administration ideas could quickly wreck a university. Direct and carefully prepared statements about educational ventures, on the other hand, can lead only to fruitful debate. After all, a president is, or should be, in touch both with new requirements and with new ideas, and if he cannot bring them to the attention of his community, he abdicates his academic leadership.

Outside the university, the various coordinating bodies have great potential as innovating forces—assuming that coordination is not construed as an organized way to make sure that the answer is no. So far, however, the performance of supra-university groups as agents of change has not been impressive. The regional compact organizations have to keep fighting a tendency to the routine. Perhaps they feel too directly the weight of public bureaucracy, or perhaps they are too new to have achieved the necessary acceptance. The voluntary organizations, notably the CIC, appear to have more zest and imagination.

The most vigorous agents for change and innovation are the great private foundations and the federal agencies, such as the National Institutes of Health, the National Science Foundation, and the U.S. Office of Education. These federal agencies have the great advantage of being free from the direct operations that restrict the range and vision of many state educational offices. Further, the new money continually available for new ideas makes federal agencies—for the foreseeable future, at least—ex-

tremely powerful forces for change and moderniza-
tion. We are perhaps too dimly aware of the blessings
of a system that leaves the federal government free
to press for improvement and change, while the
states bear the burden of daily operating supervision
and budget-making. This freedom, it seems to me,
is the most persuasive argument for having the federal government stay out of direct responsibility. I
hope that federal officials will not overlook this advantage.

The role of the foundations as innovators has been
crucial, particularly at the program level. It is un-
likely that such major changes as area studies, the
new mathematics, and honors courses would have
gone into such speedy academic orbit if foundation
initiative and foundation backing had not been available. But foundation funds, with the exception of
those of the Ford Foundation, are becoming a
smaller and smaller fraction of the total academic
budget. The tendency, as this percentage decreases,
is that foundations will move away from institution-
wide support and even from programs and projects,
finally becoming operating institutions which use
their income for their own internal programs.
Though Ford still undertakes institutional and program support and Carnegie, Sloan, and Rockefeller
are interested in programs and projects, Russell Sage
and the Carnegie Endowment are almost entirely

out of the grant-making business. Since the budget for higher education is increasing faster than the income of foundations, foundation support can be expected to play less of a direct part in educational change.

The effect of these developments will be to shift the source of the innovative force from foundations to federal agencies and to put the foundations in increasingly severe competition with federal agencies on the program and project level. And if you don't think this is already happening, take another look at the sources of funds in your university budget!

A third area of public interest in the university system has to do with planning. The significant point about planning is that, as cost and importance of educational matters increase, decision-making moves up the hierarchical scale, and away from the educational institutions toward political structures. Let me illustrate how this rule works.

I have had occasion to refer to the 200-BEV synchrotron. When its earlier and smaller predecessors were being developed, decisions could be made substantially at the department level. With the move from low-energy to high-energy physics, decision-making climbed to the university level because larger commitments of land and budget were involved. In addition, the size both of the apparatus and of the operation required the participation and support of federal agencies with greater funds and broader technical experience. When the next generation of accelerators was conceived—10–25 BEV—the size and cost could be justified only if the facility were made available on a regional basis.

When a 200-BEV machine costing over $300 million was planned, no one even suggested that it could be run by or justified for a particular university. It was inevitable that a national consortium of universities be organized to run a national facility. Some day there will be a 1000-BEV machine on the drawing boards, and it will take an international structure to manage it and to justify the expenditure. It will almost certainly have to be a facility open to the world.

That management and decision-making go up the scale as costs and importance of a project increase is only half the story. The other half is that, as costs and importance rise, there is a tendency for decision-making to gravitate closer to the political arena. The decision to locate a 10-BEV machine at Cornell was a budget decision made at the level of the White House. It very nearly became a deeper political question involving the Senate and other regions of the country. The 200-BEV machine, on the other hand, is so large that from the outset it was immersed in the political pushes and pulls of our federal system. A great many states have submitted persuasive bids for the location of this facility. The presence of the university consortium is the only barrier that prevents most decisions—and therefore results—from turning on geographical politics rather than scientific considerations. Even in this case, it may well be that the sums involved are too large to allow decisions to be made by any other than an elected body. The whole matter is a fascinating case study of the impact of cost and size on the levels and the locus of decision-making.

This raises a final point about planning. If planning now requires the participation of larger and more comprehensive organizations, then universities will have to modify their instincts for autonomy and take their places as full partners in these new planning agencies. If they do not, the inevitable consequence will be that planning and coordination will be performed by an exclusively political body.

This is the complicated balance of considerations facing all systems of higher education. It explains precisely the current dilemma of the University of California. If the drive to decentralize the seven campuses goes too far, President Kerr may not be able to convince the California government that unnecessary duplication has been removed. And if the government is not satisfied on this point, it will make its own appraisal. Thus the price of too much decentralization will be to create an administrative vacuum within the educational hierarchy—a vacuum which will inevitably be filled by political authority. Too little decentralization will keep the central power in academic hands, but the price will be paralysis on the individual campuses. It will require considerable statesmanship to understand clearly the dangers of either extreme solution.

What has been said about California holds true for the whole system of higher education. Those who want academic direction to remain in academic hands have no choice, it seems to me, but to learn how to balance their desires for independence with the necessities for close university collaboration. The only alternative will be a far more direct intervention in university affairs by government agencies. And none of us look comfortably on that prospect.

Finally, we must mention the responsibility for the integration of teaching, research, and public service. Has any agency above the level of the university established a claim to perform this task better than the university? The answer is clearly no. The specialized agencies have important roles to play in helping the university to find answers to one or another of its activites or requirements. But testing, faculty pensions, student mobility, fellowships and scholarships, coordination, planning, and the stimulation of change—none of these activities is as central to the management of knowledge as is the essential work of the university. The university remains one level in the new educational hierarchy—but it is the decisive level.

The moral of our story is that the university's decisive role leads not to isolation but to leadership, not to autonomy but rather to participation in all levels of academic organization. As the one institution in the hierarchy of education where the main business of education is centered, the university must be the chief participant, the quarterback, the leader in the whole system of higher education. For the health of the system turns largely on the vitality and health of the university, located in the middle of the entire scheme. And in order to maintain the university's vitality, those who work in the university must increasingly conduct themselves as members of a much larger community and as participants in activities at all levels of the system.

For all of us in the university there are new rules of the game. One of the most important is that the old pitting of faculty against administration must be recognized as a quaint reflection of an outmoded idea of the university. The lines between teacher and administrator will be increasingly blurred, and status will be less important than the possession of vision, range, and the creative imagination to understand how the university must change and grow if it is to play its proper part.

The new university leaders must recognize these requirements. Campus-located but system-oriented, they will have a firm grip on what is required for the pursuit of knowledge, and they will, at the same time, appreciate how each part of the system contributes to this pursuit. They will be sensitive to the philosophic dilemmas of our secular world and will understand what Wolfgang Köhler has called "the place of value in a world of fact." They will not resent the necessity for curbing isolated ambitions in the face of state, regional, national, or international interests. They will recognize that higher education is now the proper concern of every man who wishes his country well. They will know, then, that it is their rare privilege, as university men, to be at a point of great influence in their society, and that they must work to knit their university together in a manner that will support the larger interests of society.

This is no small assignment. We are asking of these new leaders more than we have ever asked of our educators before—to stand higher, see farther, and act with more wisdom. We do so because the university—the institution that now dares to accept Toynbee's challenge to make the benefits of civilization available to the whole human race—deserves the very best the country has to offer.